WHY WE LOVE SWIMMING

BLACK RABBIT BOOKS

AIDAN WHITCOMB

TABLE OF CONTENTS

1

Swimming's Start

Swimming is an old sport. People swam thousands of years ago. In time, people wanted to measure who was the best. Races were held. In 1846, the first swimming championship took place in Australia.

Today, swimming is still a big sport. Many places have pools. Millions of athletes around the world swim in races. Big events like the Olympics bring in new fans. The fastest swimmers are amazing to watch. They zip through the water!

Did You Know?

There are four competitive swimming **strokes**.

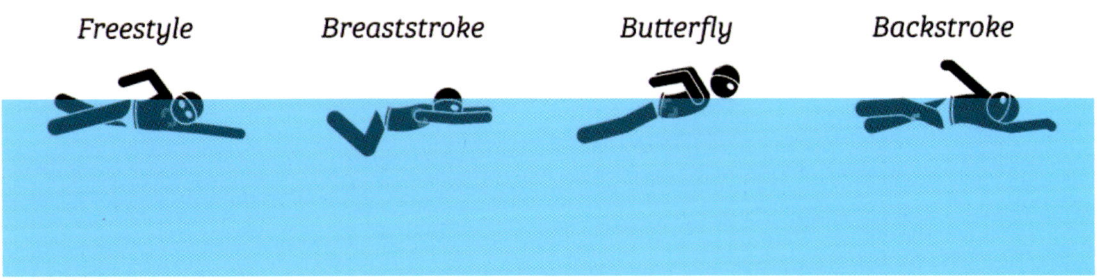

2

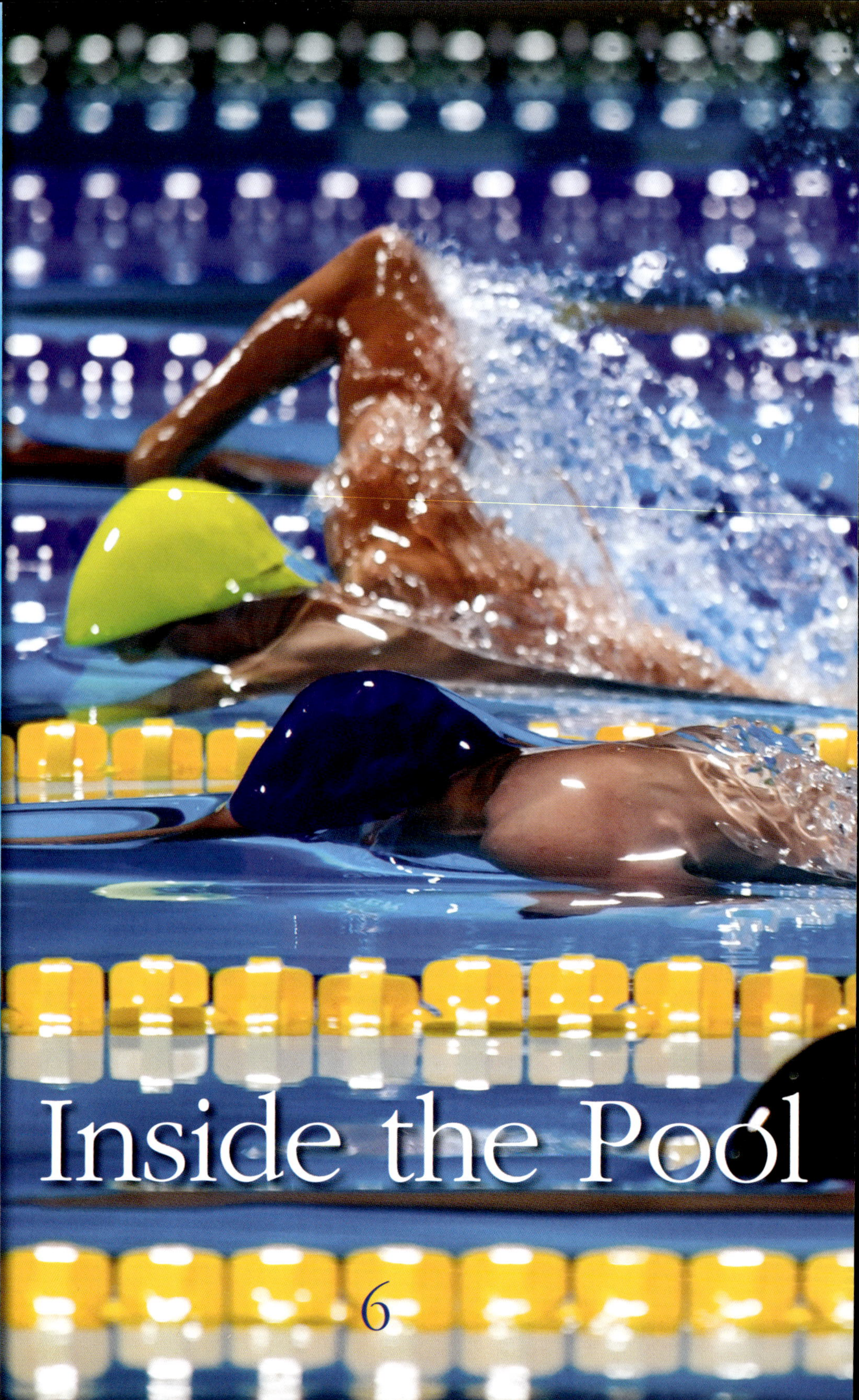

Inside the Pool

Swim meets are exciting! Indoor pools get very loud. It gets warm too. Fans fill the seats. They cheer for their favorite swimmers. Some swimmers greet fans. Sometimes fans can get autographs.

Big events can take multiple days. First, swimmers try to qualify. Then they race in the finals. Swimmers are very focused. Fans watch on the edge of their seats. A swimmer could win by a tenth of a second. Fans feel the excitement!

Did You Know?

More than 285,000 fans attended the 2024 US Olympic Swimming Trials. That is the largest swim meet ever!

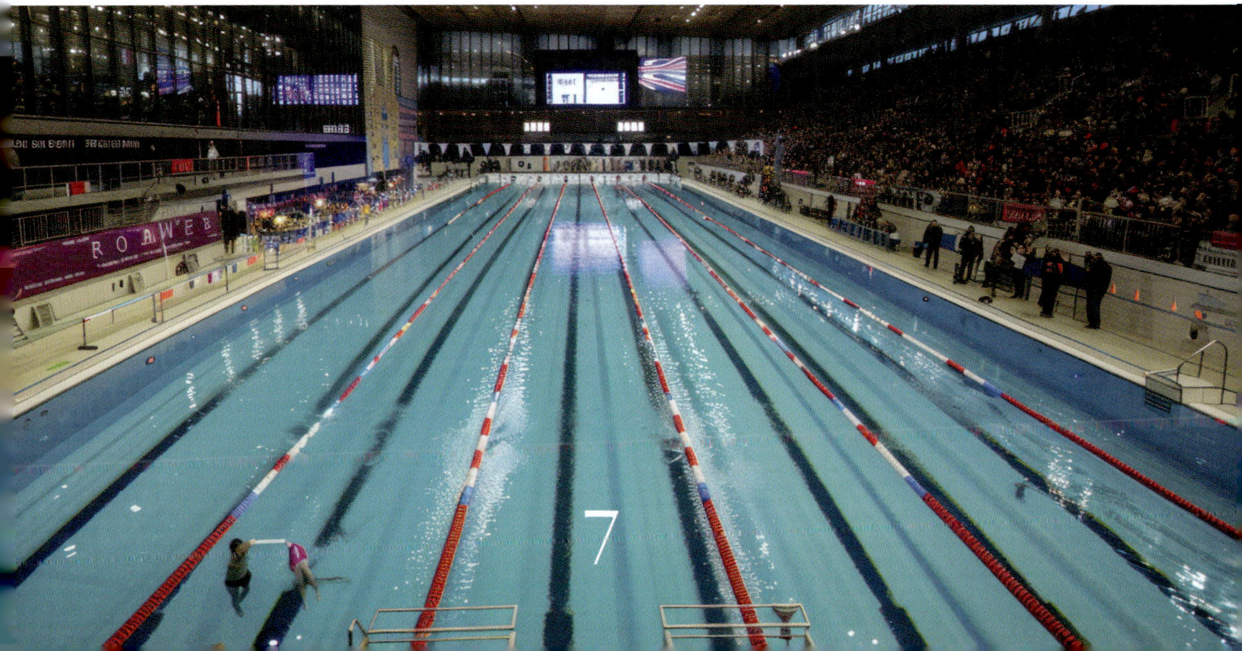

3

Katie Ledecky

Superstar Swimmers

There have been many great swimmers. The greatest female swimmer of all time is Katie Ledecky. She won a gold medal at the 2012 Olympics. She was only 15! Since then, Ledecky has rarely lost. She has nine Olympic gold medals. She has broken 16 world records.

Michael Phelps is the best male swimmer ever. He has 28 Olympic medals. That's a world record! Twenty-three are gold. Phelps set 39 world records during his career. Many fans call him the **GOAT**.

Think About It What does it take to swim in the Olympics?

Michael Phelps

4

Olympic Excitement

Léon Marchand

Swimming is very popular in the Olympics. There are 37 swimming events. Thousands of fans attend each one. They bring energy to the events.

The 2024 Olympics took place in Paris, France. French swimmer Léon Marchand was one of the best. The French fans went wild at all his races. They chanted his name. He won four gold medals!

Kyoko Iwasaki

Did You Know?
Kyoko Iwasaki is the youngest swimmer to win Olympic gold at age 14 in 1992.

5

The World Championships

The World Championships is the largest swimming tournament. It is held every two years. Thousands of swimmers battle for the title. There are 47 events.

The World Championships have been held in 15 countries. Fans from all over the world pack the pool. The events are loud and entertaining!

Did You Know?

The United States has the most World Championship medals. Australia and China are second and third.

6

Open Water Swimming

Open water swimming is an outdoor sport. Athletes swim in oceans, lakes, or rivers. These races are long. Swimmers need endurance. They swim for miles (kilometers). The water can be rough and cold. Fans love to watch these extreme events.

Thomas Lurz is one of the best of all time. He is German. He has won seven Open Water World Championships! Ana Marcela Cunha is a great female distance swimmer. She is from Brazil. She won Olympic gold in 2021. She has won 29 Open Swim World Cups!

Think About It

What challenges do open water swimmers face compared to indoor swimmers?

Thomas Lurz

MORE TO EXPLORE

FANTASTIC FACTS

Olympic-sized pools hold about 660,000 gallons (2.5 million liters) of water. That is enough for 9,400 baths!

Alfréd Hajós won the first-ever Olympic swimming gold medal.

Cesar Cielo holds the 50m freestyle world record. He swam it in just 20.91 seconds!

Katie Ledecky has all 20 of the fastest women's 1500m freestyle times.

The longest swimming race is 54.6 miles (88 kilometers).

Swimming burns more calories than biking and running.

MORE TO EXPLORE

COOL COMPARISONS

Which countries have the most Olympic swimming medals?

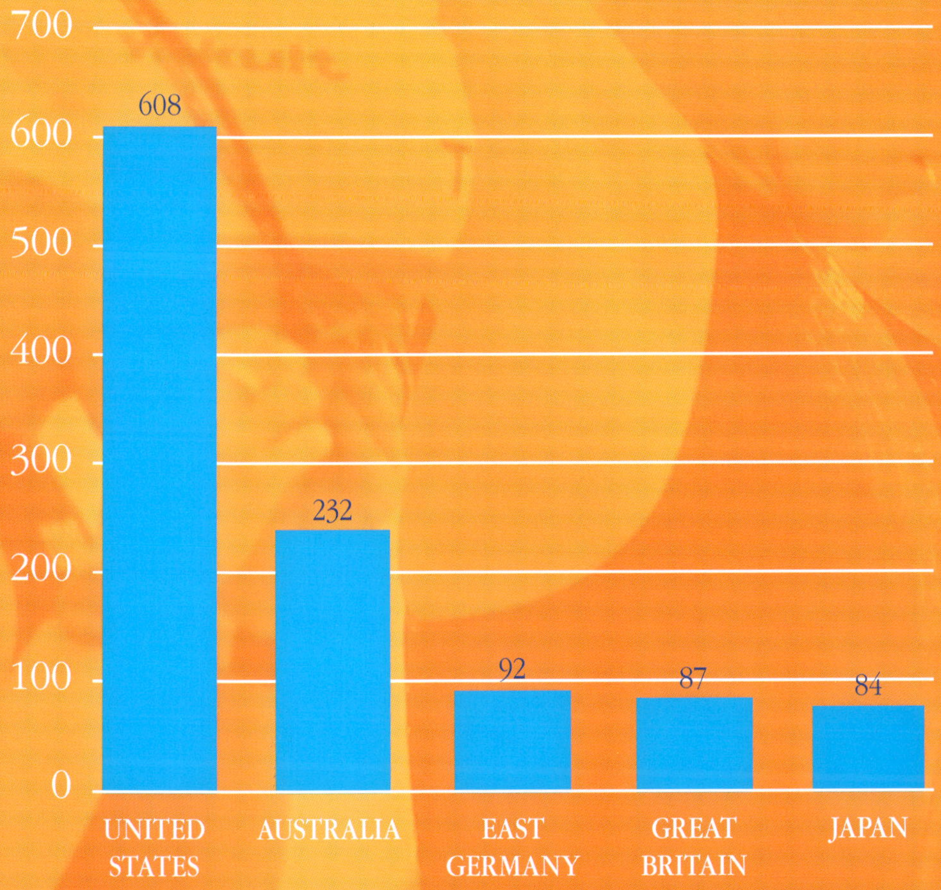

MORE TO EXPLORE

RESOURCES

Glossary

autograph (AW-tuh-grahf) The signature of a famous person.

endurance (en-DOOR-uhns) The ability to do something difficult for a long time.

GOAT (GOHT) A person who is excellent or the best in their field; GOAT stands for "greatest of all time.".

meet (MEET) A large gathering of athletes for a sports competition.

qualify (KWOL-uh-fahy) To have the necessary skills or knowledge to do something.

stroke (STROHK) A series of repeated swimming movements to move through the water.

Read More

Bolte, Mari. *Aquatics*. Mankato, MN: Creative Education and Creative Paperbacks, 2024.

Tischler, Joe. *Katie Ledecky*. Mankato, MN: Amicus Learning, 2025.

Index

TOP RANK is published by Black Rabbit Books, P.O. Box 227, Mankato, MN, 56002.

• Top Rank is an imprint of Black Rabbit Books. • Designed by Danny Nanos • Photographs © Associated Press/Kirsty Wigglesworth, cover, 1, Dreamstime/Kristina Kuptsevich, 13, Si Le, 7, Walter Arce, 12–13; Freepik/BG_illustrations, cover, 1; Getty Images/Al Bello, 15, Attila Kisbenedek, 21, Clive Rose, 20, 23, OLI SCARFF, 8–9, Toshifumi Kitamura, 14; Shutterstock/BrunoRosa, 6, fifg, 10, Focus Pix, 2, 11, 18, Jacob Lund, 19, Leremy, 5, Oleksandr Nagaiets, 16–17, PeopleImages.com - Yuri A, 4 • Printed in India.

Library of Congress Cataloging-in-Publication Data: Names: Whitcomb, Aidan, author. | Title: Why we love swimming / by Aidan Whitcomb. | Description: Mankato, MN : Top Rank, an imprint of Black Rabbit Books, 2026. | Series: Why we love sports | Includes bibliographical references and index. | Audience: Ages 8–11 | Audience: Grades 2–3 | Identifiers: LCCN 2024050022 (print) | LCCN 2024050023 (ebook) | ISBN 9781644668085 (library binding) | ISBN 9781644668405 (paperback) | ISBN 9781644668726 (ebook) | Subjects: LCSH: Swimming—Juvenile literature. | Classification: LCC GV837.6 .W525 2026 (print) | LCC GV837.6 (ebook) | DDC 797.2/1—dc23/eng/20241129 | LC record available at https://lccn.loc.gov/2024050022